THE LITTLE
BLACK BOOK OF

COFFEE

The Essential Guide to
Your Favorite Perk-Me-Up

KAREN BERMAN

ILLUSTRATED BY KERREN BARBAS

PETER PAUPER PRESS, INC.
WHITE PLAINS, NEW YORK

IN MEMORY OF MY MOTHER, JANICE,
WHO LOVED A GOOD CUP OF COFFEE

*With thanks to my dear Oscar, for help preparing
the manuscript. Thanks, also, to Evelyn L. Beilenson,
Ruth Cullen, Virginia Reynolds, Claire Criscuolo,
Geri Ficarra, and Francine Fielding,
who developed many of the recipes in this book, and
to Keith E. Davis, who provided a personal coffee tutorial.
And to the thoughtful and caring editors at
Peter Pauper Press, a heartfelt thank you, as well.*

Designed by Heather Zschock

Illustrations copyright © 2006 Kerren Barbas

Visit us at www.peterpauper.com

THE LITTLE
BLACK BOOK OF
COFFEE

CONTENTS

introduction

*I think we all pray to the first cup of the day.
It's a silent prayer, sung while the mind is
still foggy and blue. "O Magic Cup,"
it might go, "carry me above the traffic jam.
Keep me civil in the subway. And forgive
my employer, as you forgive me. Amen"*

STEWART LEE ALLEN

Perhaps you grind your own coffee beans from a thoughtfully selected blend, brew them up with distilled water, pour the resulting liquor into a special mug and—ahhh—savor each mouthful. Or maybe you pop a pod into the coffeemaker, fill up your travel mug, and hotfoot it out the door. Then again, you might hand over some bucks for a half-caf tall latte with two-percent milk, and then dress it with half a pack of sweetener and a sprinkle of cinnamon.

Whatever your ideal cup, it's nice now and then, as you take that welcome first sip, to ponder coffee: where it came from, how it got to you, and how it is that people all over the world, whether richer or poorer than you, younger or older, smarter or not so smart, share your devotion to these seemingly common grounds. Coffee punctuates

our days; it helps us wake up in the morning, signals a break in the workday, keeps us alert through the afternoon, and then, in the evening, helps us prolong the pleasure of dinner and conversation.

But coffee's reach goes far beyond the realm of the personal. It has been at the center of religious rituals in some cultures and banned by the clergy in others. It's been served as a sign of aristocracy and as a balm to extreme hunger. It's been a justification for slavery and a lubricant of revolutions. Today, coffee is the planet's second most frequently traded commodity after oil. Worldwide, about $80 billion is spent on it annually, and more than 20 million souls derive a livelihood from it.

Indeed, submerged in your morning cup, along with the milk or cream, sugar or artifi-

cial sweetener, or whatever your preference, is nothing less than the full course of human events.

A Short History of Coffee

Nobody knows the exact origin of coffee, but scholars place it in the mountainous rainforest of what is now Ethiopia, sometime before the 10th century A.D. Legend has it that coffee was "discovered" by a goatherd named Kaldi, or, rather, by his goats. One day, when the goats did not come in response to his piped call, Kaldi found them romping in a frenzy, nibbling the berries and leaves of a bush that he did not recognize. The next day, satisfied that the goats hadn't poisoned themselves—they ran directly to the same bush and began eating and dancing again—he tried chewing on the strange leaves and berries himself. Soon he was dancing, too.

The world's first coffee lovers didn't drink coffee as we know it, but chewed the leaves and berries; infused them in hot water like tea; ground them and mixed them with animal fat for a snack; or made a sort of wine when the berries fermented. Roasting and grinding the beans and brewing the result in hot water to make coffee as we do today probably began sometime between the 13th and 16th centuries.

With time, traders and kidnapped slaves carried coffee beyond Ethiopia. To the east across the Red Sea, it was embraced in what is now Yemen, and by the 15th century that area had become a locus of coffee cultivation. The port city of al-Makkha, or Mocha, gave the bean a nickname that has stuck to this day, although the city has long ceased to be a coffee center. It might have been there, too, that the root of the word coffee emerged. Some called it *qahwah,* Arabic for wine; this is believed to have evolved into the word coffee.

Sufi Muslim holy men who traveled throughout the Arab world probably brought coffee with them, as it enabled them to stay awake for midnight prayers. Some Sufis, better known to the world as whirling dervishes, incorporated coffee into their religious devotions, first sharing a pot and then spinning in place to arrive at a state of prayerful intoxication. Soon coffee became a secular drink taken at home and in coffeehouses, a trend that established its importance as a trading commodity even then.

The Ottoman Empire's conquest of coffee-rich Yemen and its expansion throughout northern Africa, the Middle East, and Europe made coffee a staple of all those societies. The Ottoman Turks understood full well the value of the coffee crop, and forbade trade in fertile berries or seedlings. The ban was violated, of course, and in the 1600s, seeds were smuggled to India. Seedlings traveled to Southeast Asia at the close of the century via Dutch traders. Their cultivation of coffee in Java, in what is now Indonesia, gave the beverage yet another nickname.

In the 18th century, the bean arrived in the New World, although it's unclear if it was first established there by the Dutch, the Portuguese, or the French. Whether he was actually the first to bring coffee plants to the New World, a French nobleman named Gabriel De Clieu is celebrated for his role in coffee's arrival in the Americas. In 1720, he smuggled a coffee plant to the French colony of Martinique, sharing his limited water supply with the seedling on a perilous ocean voyage. Today, much of Latin America's coffee crop can probably trace its lineage to De Clieu's plant. Coffee cultivation

 was introduced to neighboring Caribbean islands such as Haiti, and to equatorial regions of Central and South

America, in what is now Brazil, Colombia, Guatemala, Nicaragua, and El Salvador, as well as Mexico.

The large-scale cultivation of coffee under unimaginably harsh conditions required an ample labor force. In the Dutch-controlled coffee plantations of Java, enslaved Javanese did the job. In the Americas, coffee was cultivated and processed by enslaved Africans (who performed the same function on sugar plantations); indigenous Native Americans forced into virtual serfdom as their lands were commandeered for coffee; and indentured laborers from Europe, who generally fled the plantations as soon as they were able. And no wonder—sadly, conditions for coffee workers wherever they came from were routinely made more miserable by plantation owners who paid them little or nothing and worked them like beasts. Haiti's slave revolt of 1791, led by Toussaint L'Ouverture, was provoked by the conditions suffered by coffee plantation workers.

While the great trading nations were attempting to cultivate coffee in far-flung corners of the world where the climate and elevation were conducive to the new crop, coffee as a commodity to be roasted, ground, and brewed was also making its way around the globe. It arrived in Europe in the 17th century, traveling by a variety of routes. The expanding Ottoman Empire introduced coffee throughout what is now Eastern Europe, and trade along the Spice Route carried it to Venice. Ironically, coffee's journey to Europe was further encouraged by a Turkish sultan's ban on it. (This was not the first prohibition of coffee. Much earlier, in the 16th century, even as its popularity was spreading in the Islamic world, several Muslim holy men had banned it on the grounds that it was used, like wine, as an intoxicant.) This time, however, the sultan's objections concerned the coffeehouse, which he feared as a breeding ground of revolution. Deprived of their venue, the empire's coffee sellers took their wares elsewhere.

In London, the coffeehouse became a place for people to congregate and for businessmen to transact their business. Some coffeehouses catered to specific industries. Edward Lloyd's coffeehouse was a gathering place for maritime traders and their insurers. Lloyd's eventually gave up coffee and became one of the best-known insurance companies in the world, Lloyd's of London.

In what is now Italy, the appearance of coffee alarmed the clergy, who asked Pope Clement VIII to ban it. He insisted on tasting it first, and when he did, he liked it so well he gave it his papal approval. Elsewhere, coffee was sold along with lemonade, on the street, and later, in *caffes*. The color of the Capuchin

 monks' robes led to the name cappuccino.

Coffee came to Paris near the end of the 17th century, when the Ottoman Empire was preparing to invade Vienna. Hoping to secure a nonaggression pact with France, Ottoman rulers sent an ambassador to Paris. By this time the Turkish ban on coffee was a memory and the ambassador made a habit of entertaining the French aristocracy with lavish coffee parties held in silk tents with gold and silver coffee service. The ambassador was rewarded with his treaty, and within a few years, the café had become a fixture of the city. The French Revolution is said to have been conceived in a café, and since then the institution has been beloved by French artists, intellectuals, laborers, businessmen, and tourists alike.

In 1683, the Ottoman leaders sent their armies to try to take Vienna, the capital of the rival Hapsburg Empire. That attempt ended with a devastating retreat and, in the process, the fleeing Ottoman troops left behind bags of coffee beans, inadvertently giving rise to the famed Viennese coffeehouse.

Germany acquired a taste for coffee in the late 1600s and early 1700s. In 1732, Johann Sebastian Bach wrote his *Coffee Cantata*, a humorous work in which a daughter tells her father that coffee is "lovelier than a thousand kisses." As German farmers followed the Industrial Revolution into the cities, their wives—who were consequently freed from the sun-up-till-sundown labors of the farmer's wife—became fond of their *kaffeeklatsch* (a gathering at which they exchanged views and gossip).

Across Europe, newly minted industrial workers drank coffee to stave off hunger pangs that arose during their long hours in the factories.

In the English colonies of America, the crown's tax on tea prompted the Boston Tea Party, a famous event in which a group of colonists, dressed as Native Americans, dumped tea waiting to be unloaded from three cargo ships into Boston Harbor. Less well known is that the colonials drank coffee thereafter.

So did the nation that rose in their place, as did much of the rest of the world. Coffee became the subject of political schemes and financial machinations, of scientific study and marketing madness. And for the past century it has been part of the daily life of untold millions.

THE BOTANY OF COFFEE

What we call the coffee bean is actually a seed found inside the fruit of the coffee tree. Coffee grows best in a region called the coffee belt, an area that rings the globe, within 25° to 30° latitudes north and south of the equator. Once planted, it takes three to four years for the tree to bear fruit.

The fruit, known as the coffee cherry, contains two seeds, each encased in a thin skin, which are in turn surrounded by a parchment-like covering.

For all the fuss about different kinds of coffee these days, there are only two botanical varieties of bean that account for the coffee we drink: arabica and robusta.

Arabica is the bean of ancient Ethiopia, prized for its rich flavor and enticing aroma. It grows best at higher equatorial altitudes, where the temperature fluctuations are thought to improve the flavor and aroma of the bean.

Robusta beans were discovered in 1898 in what was then the Belgian Congo. Hardier, tolerant of lower altitudes, and resistant to leaf rust, robusta beans are higher in caffeine than arabicas, but comparatively harsh and bitter in flavor—so much so that for a time, they were barred from trading by the New York Coffee Exchange.

A hybrid of the two, known as the caturra plant, is a hardy specimen, but it produces coffee that is not considered high quality.

THE ART OF TASTING

Coffee is sometimes compared with wine, in that in both several components work together to create an overall flavor. Although the evaluation of coffee, known as cupping, has yet to achieve a language or a ratings system as popular with the general public as those used for wine tasting, professional coffee tasters have developed their own lexicon for evaluating the characteristics of the brew.

AROMA: The scent of brewed coffee. Typical descriptors include strong, moderate, delicate, faint, floral, nutty, spicy, and fragrant. Aroma is the coffee drinker's first sensory experience of a cup of coffee. (Some coffee experts differentiate further, between fragrance—the smell of ground beans—and aroma—the smell of ground coffee that has steeped in water.

Some add yet another characteristic, the "nose" of the coffee, which refers to the vapors the coffee releases in the mouth.)

ACIDITY: The pleasing tartness of a coffee. Acidity in coffee does not mean sourness or sharpness.

BODY: The quality of richness—or lack thereof—that a coffee imparts in the mouth, often known as mouthfeel. Commonly used descriptors of body include full, medium, thin, and slight, as well as buttery, oily, or rich.

FLAVOR: The taste or character of the coffee—how the various components come together in a complex, balanced whole. Positive descriptors include earthy, winy, nutty, spicy, cinnamony, toasty, and tangy.

 Negative descriptors include harsh, bitter, green, grassy, strawy, hidey (as in leather), muddy, woody, rancid, rubbery, and musty.

FINISH: The aftertaste—that is, the taste remaining in the mouth after swallowing a coffee, much like the finish described by wine tasters. A coffee's finish is often related to its body; the fuller the body, the longer the finish.

JAVA GEOGRAPHY

Coffee is grown around the world, on four continents and in more than 50 countries. Because of the differences in climate, elevation, soil, and water, as well as variations in weather from year to year, each nation's coffee has a distinct character. Indeed, each region within a coffee-growing nation can produce its own signature bean.

THE AMERICAS

BRAZIL is the world's top coffee producer. A

significant part of its coffee crop consists of robusta beans that are grown at lower elevations, although the more highly regarded arabicas are also grown in Brazil. Much Brazilian coffee ends up as instant coffee or lesser canned coffees; while some is used for espresso. The typical Brazilian cup is medium-bodied, slightly sweet, clear, and low in acid. Its better grades, especially the one known as Bourbon Santos, are highly prized and typically described as well-balanced and mildly acidic.

COLOMBIA, long the second-largest coffee producer in the world, makes high-quality coffee that is known for its consistency. The flavor is described as medium- to full-bodied, with good acidity and slightly sweet, caramel, and winy notes. Colombian supremo, the arabica bean grown at the highest elevations, is considered this nation's best.

GUATEMALA'S midland mountain region grows long, bluish  coffee beans that make distinctively flavored, well-balanced, aromatic coffee, often with spicy or chocolaty notes. The nation's coffee-growing areas are noted for their volcanic soils and numerous microclimates. Antigua is the coffee-growing region most familiar to outsiders, while coffee from Cobán is known for its smoky quality.

VENEZUELA produces coffee that is similar to Colombian coffee. The most familiar is Maracaibo, named for the port from which it is shipped. Mérida is a lower-acid, slightly sweet coffee.

COSTA RICA produces beautifully balanced medium-bodied coffees that are nicely acidic. Some call them delicate. The country's coffee industry is known for its careful processing.

JAMAICA is famous for Jamaica Blue Mountain Coffee, an expensive brew that is mellow, with sweet notes and lovely aroma. Other varieties are High Mountain Supreme and Prime Jamaica Washed; these are considered very nice, but not as good as Blue Mountain. Beware of coffees labeled as Blue Mountain blends that are in fact made from completely different coffees.

PUERTO RICO was once a major coffee producer, but its industry was devastated by hurricanes and global competition. In recent years, the island has seen a coffee revival, and high-quality Puerto Rican beans have returned to the market. Puerto Rican coffee is characterized by fruity aroma and balanced body and acidity.

MEXICO'S best-known coffees are grown in its southern regions, largely in the states of Oaxaca, Veracruz and Chiapas. The large beans from these regions yield brews that are light-bodied, acidic, and aromatic. Some have hazelnut notes. If Mexican coffee is labeled as *altura*, it was grown at a higher elevation.

AFRICA/MIDDLE EAST

ETHIOPIAN coffee is typically gathered wild, and not cultivated. It is described as bold and very acidic. The eastern part of the country produces coffee with a near-fermented flavor, while the south produces a more floral cup.

YEMEN, the world's first commercial coffee producer and once its coffee capital, produces coffees called Mochas in honor of the ancient port of that name. Mochas are rich, with a chocolaty finish. Some say they resemble the Ethiopian coffees found just across the Red Sea. In an arid land where water is a scarce resource, Mochas are produced in limited quantities, and can be hard to come by in the West, although they can be found in Mocha-Java blends. Beware, though, as these blends often contain a high proportion of lesser quality beans.

KENYA produces high-quality coffee with its own national grading system based on size and other factors. (The largest beans are known as Kenyan AA.) Kenyan coffee is full-bodied, with fruity acidity, and a rich fragrance. The finish can be winy, as in Kenyan AA beans, or sour, as in Kenyan Bs.

ZIMBABWE'S coffees are similar to Kenya's but slightly less intense.

TANZANIA is known for coffee that grows in single seeds, or peaberries, which produce a rich yet simple brew with delicate acidity. The beans are grown on the slopes of Mount Kilimanjaro and other peaks.

IVORY COAST is one of the top robusta-growing regions in the world. Light-bodied and aromatic, they are often roasted very dark and used in espresso.

ASIA/PACIFIC RIM

INDONESIA is the source of some of the world's most prized coffees, known for their full body, mild acidity, syrupy richness, and spicy character. Its coffees are typically named for the island where they are grown and each has a distinctive character. Sumatra produces dark, rich brews, while Java serves up coffees with medium body, nice acidity, and a short, creamy finish. Sulawesi, once known as Celebes, produces balanced coffees with lively acidity but less body. Indonesia is also known for aged coffees. Storing the coffee in the islands' uniquely moist, tropical climate creates a brew with less acidity and deeper body.

HAWAII'S best-known coffee is grown in the Kona region of the island of Hawaii, at lower altitudes than other coffee-growing areas; but the island's climate is much like the typical higher coffee region.

This produces coffee that is medium-bodied, with good acidity, lovely aroma, and notes of wine, cinnamon and clove. Kona coffee is among the most expensive coffee in the world. Beware Kona blends, which usually contain a high proportion of lesser coffees.

VIETNAM is fast becoming one of the world's largest coffee producers. Most of its beans are the robusta variety, and wind up in blended coffees. Vietnamese coffee tends to be mild-bodied, lightly acidic, with good balance.

INDIA'S coffees tend to be full-bodied and deep, yet delicate. Some have spicy notes.

THE CONSCIENCE OF COFFEE

Wherever it takes place, coffee cultivation is a backbreaking, arduous undertaking that, because of the tropical climates and high elevations involved, defies attempts to fully mechanize it. And the hard lot of coffee farmers the world over has been made even worse by low coffee prices that have persisted for the past 50 years; often they are lower than the cost of production. Whether employed by large plantations or working their own small family farms, those who tend the coffee tree and pick its fruit have long eked out the barest of livelihoods. And with the farmer's pay based on the number of bags picked, many have been obliged to have their children work alongside them.

In the 1980s, when the specialty coffee movement

spawned new interest in how coffee is produced, the lot of the coffee farmer came before the world stage and the concept of "fair trade" coffee was born. Fair trade coffee is sold for more than market price, and the difference is paid to the farmer. Identifiable by the fair trade logo imprinted on each package, fair trade coffee is more expensive than other coffees. Early on, it was largely available from specialty retailers, in co-ops and by mail, but in recent years, several major retailers have begun to sell it. To date, it has captured only a fraction of the coffee market, but it represents a move toward redressing the social inequities created by coffee.

At the same time that the human cost of

coffee production began to attract attention, so, too, did the environmental cost. Coffee typically flourishes as a shade crop; its trees thrive under the canopy provided by taller trees, which also offer a habitat to numerous species of migratory birds and other wildlife. The last decades of the 20th century saw the development of hybrid coffee varieties that could grow in full sun in tightly crowded rows. In some Latin American countries, growers adopted these hybrids, clearing the rainforests and in the process decimating the bird population. Deforestation also caused soil erosion and deprived coffee farms of a natural source of mulch, wind barriers, and drought protection. And the result, full-sun coffee, is considered an inferior product by many coffee experts.

In response to concerns voiced by environmentalists, some coffee producers and sellers have begun to label "shade coffee" or "sustainable coffee," made from beans cultivated in the shade of the remaining forests. It, too, constitutes a fraction of the coffee market, but is a step toward recognition that the inexpensive cup we enjoy each day comes at a cost beyond that found in our wallets.

PROCESSING AND ROASTING

Once picked, coffee cherries are highly perishable, so they must be processed as soon as possible. Some coffee growers use the traditional dry method, in which the cherries are spread out to dry in the sun and turned several times a day. Drying can take several weeks.

Some coffee growers opt for the wet method, in which the pulp of the coffee cherry is removed from the beans by a machine that transports them through a conveyor of water. The water washes away the coffee cherry pulp and separates the beans by weight, with the heavier beans sinking to the

 bottom. The beans are then held in a water tank for up to two days, during which time the mucilage that surrounds them dissolves and the beans

ferment. The fermented beans are then dried in the sun or in automated tumblers.

The processed beans are shipped to warehouses where they are hulled. For wet-processed beans, hulling removes the parchment layer that still surrounds them. For dry-processed beans, the whole husk—mucilage, parchment, and everything else that remains—is removed. Once hulled, the beans are graded and sorted. At this stage, the coffee is considered "green coffee" and is shipped to the coffee-consuming country where it will be prepared for market.

When they reach their destination, the green coffee beans are roasted to an internal temperature of 400° to 500°. This process is vital to the creation of coffee as we know it. The heat releases the beans' volatile oils and transforms their complex chemical components into starch and sugar, creating the flavors and aromas we identify with coffee. If the coffee were simply cooked in hot water without roasting, the resulting brew would not taste like coffee.

The intensity of the roast is yet another factor in the character of the coffee. Much of the coffee produced in the U.S. gets a light to medium roast. The lightest treatment is known straightforwardly as light roast, but also as cinnamon roast, institutional roast, New England roast, or half city roast. This produces coffee with a mild, somewhat acidic flavor, slight body, and a light brown hue. Medium, also called American roast, Breakfast roast, or regular roast, yields coffee that is lightly sweet and rich, yet still acidic. The color is medium brown. City and full city roast are darker, richer, with little acidity. Dark-roasted coffee, also called Viennese, continental, or New Orleans roast, is darker in color and has a smoky, sweet taste on the tongue. Darker still are French and Italian roasts, but espresso roasts are the darkest, and they produce beans that are nearly black. They have a distinctly burned flavor that many coffee drinkers love and others can't abide.

Roasting typically takes only a few minutes, but it's not a simple process. Roasting that's too fast or too hot can produce scorched beans. Roasting that's too slow or not hot enough will produce coffee with a weak flavor.

Roasted beans are best fresh, so very soon after roasting, they are either packaged whole or ground and then packaged. Vacuum packaging keeps beans fresher longer.

Another processing operation that some coffee is subjected to is the removal of its naturally occurring caffeine. Caffeine is an alkaloid, a flavorless chemical component of coffee that acts as a

 stimulant, affecting the brain, the heart and circulatory system, the lungs, the digestive system, and other parts of the body in both positive and negative ways. Chief among the negatives is that it can block the chemical reaction in the brain that allows us to sleep, a quality that affects some coffee drinkers more seriously than others.

The invention of decaffeinated coffee in the early 20th century enabled coffee lovers to have their coffee and sleep, too. Several different methods are used to remove caffeine from coffee beans, by treating them with chemical solvents, water, or carbon dioxide. To greater and lesser extents, these methods also diminish the flavor and aroma of coffee, but decaffeination does provide an alternative for the legions of coffee lovers who can't tolerate too much caffeine.

One more process is necessary to prepare the beans to make coffee, and that is grinding.

Grinding exponentially enlarges the surface area of the coffee that is exposed to the hot water, and enables the water to extract flavor and aroma.

Much of the coffee sold today is pre-ground. But since the coffee revival of the 1980s, an increasingly large percentage has been sold in bean form, to be ground at home or in machines at the point of purchase.

Grinding the beans just before brewing takes time, but it affords coffee drinkers maximum flavor and aroma. Once the beans are ground, the volatile oils responsible for these qualities dissipate somewhat with time and exposure to air.

Different brewing methods require different grinds. The automatic drip coffeemaker with the flat-bottomed filter that is commonly in use today requires a medium grind, as

does the stovetop espresso maker. Fine grind is suitable for the cone-shaped filter and for vacuum pots, while very fine grind is a must for espresso, which is exposed to the hot water briefly. Percolators and French press pots can handle coarse grind.

Whether you buy pre-ground coffee or grind it yourself, the way you store coffee is important. Coffee should be stored in an airtight container in a dry, cool, dark place. Ideally, once the coffee has been exposed to the air, it should be used within two weeks. If you won't finish your coffee in that time, store it in the freezer in an airtight container for up to a month or so.

THE WORLD OF COFFEE-MAKING GEAR

There's an incredible variety of coffee-making equipment on the market today. As with the coffee itself, each type has its adherents, and many are passionate about their choice.

THE AUTOMATIC DRIP FILTER COFFEE MAKER is the most popular coffeemaker in use today. The self-contained unit heats the water to the proper temperature and automatically drips it, drop by drop, through a filter filled with ground coffee and into a carafe, which either sits on a warming plate or has thermal properties to keep the coffee warm.

These machines generally call for disposable paper filters, which come in bleached or unbleached

varieties. Others rely on reusable gold-mesh or nylon filters.

Some automatic drip machines have special features beyond the basic making of coffee. Programmable timers allow you to prep your coffeemaker at night and have coffee brewed and ready for you in the morning. Pause buttons enable you to stop the coffee from dripping into the carafe long enough for you to fill your cup. Then there are travel carafes, built-in grinders, small-batch settings, brew strength controls, automatic shut-off options, self-contained water filters—and the list of possibilities keeps getting longer.

THE POD COFFEEMAKER is the newest entrant onto the coffee-making scene. It uses packets, or pods, of pre-ground coffee that make one cup at a time. At the push of a button, the machine heats the water and forces it through the grounds under pressure, a process based on the same principle as an espresso machine. Because the coffee is encased in a pod, there's no chance of spilling grounds and making a mess, so clean up is fast and easy. Pods are designed for single-serve use, but some machines have larger capacity and can hold enough pods to brew several cups in succession.

THE FRENCH PRESS, or PLUNGER POT, consists of a glass or ceramic cylinder with a fitted plunger/filter. The coffee is placed in the bottom of the cylinder, the hot water is added, and the coffee steeps for several minutes. Then the plunger is pressed down, pushing the grounds to the bottom, effectively straining them from the coffee. It produces a rich coffee that some insist is better than that produced by the more popular automatic drip method.

THE MANUAL DRIP FILTER METHOD operates on a principle similar to the automatic drip machine. The filled filter sits in a cone-shaped holder that is perched on a coffee cup or carafe. Hot water is poured manually over the grounds and the coffee drips into the receptacle below.

THE NEAPOLITAN POT is a variation on the drip method. It consists of two metal cylinders, one atop the other, with a filter between them. The grounds go in the filter and the water goes in the bottom. The bottom is heated and when the water boils, the whole apparatus is flipped over so that the water drips through the grounds.

THE PERCOLATOR was the coffeemaker of choice during the early 20th century, before the automatic drip machine overtook it. A metal tube runs down the length of the pot, with a metal filter basket attached to it on top. The grounds are placed in the filter basket and water is boiled in the pot. The boiling water travels up the tube into the grounds. A tight lid keeps it from overflowing, and the resulting coffee filters back down into the pot, back up the rod and into the grounds again and again until the coffee is brewed. The percolator has largely fallen out of favor due to the ease of the automatic drip machine and the fact that it can give the coffee a boiled quality, but a contingent of coffee drinkers still uses it.

THE VACUUM POT consists of two glass chambers with a filter between them. The water is boiled in the bottom one and ground coffee sits in the other. When the water boils, it is forced into the top chamber, where the coffee steeps. When the pot is removed from the heat, a vacuum is formed in the lower chamber and the coffee is sucked back down into it, the grounds strained out by the screen between the chambers. The bottom chamber then serves as a carafe. Some coffee lovers think the vacuum pot produces superior coffee, but this product of 19th-century technology can be fragile and is not widely used today.

THE JEZVE or IBRIK is a brass or copper pot with a long handle that is traditional in the Middle East and Turkey. The handle is a vestige of the days when the coffee was brewed over an open fire. Ground coffee, water, sugar, and, often, spices are placed into it and boiled until thick and frothy. The resulting coffee is served in demitasse cups. The grounds sometimes find their way into the cup and the coffee drinker must avoid downing them with the coffee.

COLD-WATER BREWING steeps the coffee without heating it. Grounds are steeped in cold water for 10 to 24 hours, and filtered to make a sort of coffee concentrate. Based on an age-old Peruvian custom, cold-brewed coffee is lower in acidity than its hot counterpart because it extracts fewer acids and oils. To drink it hot, you add hot water. You can also use it for iced coffee. Unlike hot brews, which are best drunk immediately, it can keep well in the refrigerator for approximately two to three weeks.

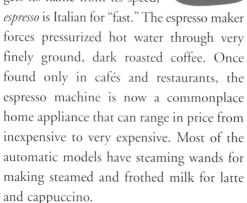

THE ESPRESSO MACHINE

gets its name from its speed; *espresso* is Italian for "fast." The espresso maker forces pressurized hot water through very finely ground, dark roasted coffee. Once found only in cafés and restaurants, the espresso machine is now a commonplace home appliance that can range in price from inexpensive to very expensive. Most of the automatic models have steaming wands for making steamed and frothed milk for latte and cappuccino.

THE STOVETOP ESPRESSO POT is a

"manual" espresso maker consisting of a two-chambered pot. The top chamber has a spout. The bottom is filled with water, which when brought to a boil, rises through a filter containing the finely ground coffee, and into the top chamber. The resulting espresso is poured through the spout into demitasse cups.

In addition to coffee makers, you can choose from several kinds of coffee grinders. The most common is the electric grinder with a rotating blade. It is fast and inexpensive. Some coffee lovers prefer the coffee mill, either electric or manual. It crushes the beans between metal plates, which, because they are adjustable, give the user excellent control over the coarseness or fineness of the beans.

THE HEALTH EFFECTS OF COFFEE

Coffee has been demonized as a threat to good health almost since its earliest use. Early critics denounced it, wrongly, as an intoxicant. In the 19th and 20th centuries it was blamed for "coffee nerves" and linked with everything from cancer to heart disease. Many of these claims have never been proven.

Of course, the caffeine in coffee does, in some people, affect brain chemistry and interfere with sleep. And it can also stimulate the heart and circulatory system— a risk for those with high blood pressure and/or coronary disease.

In recent years, however, medical research has indicated that coffee actually has several health benefits. Studies have shown that it lowers the risk of type 2 diabetes, liver disease, colorectal cancers, Parkinson's disease, and gall bladder disease, and can help manage asthma and migraine and other headaches. It can also boost physical performance and endurance. Researchers believe these findings are linked to the numerous antioxidants and phytoestrogens in coffee, as well as to its magnesium content.

hot coffee drinks

*The morning cup of coffee has an exhilaration
about it which the cheering influence of the
afternoon or evening cup of tea cannot
be expected to reproduce.*

OLIVER WENDELL HOLMES, SR.

There's a whole world in your coffee cup—history, geography, science, technology, folklore, fantasy—but in the end, when you lift it to your lips, it's all about a good cup o' joe. What makes that good cup? That's the beauty part: it's up to you to decide. The recipes that follow will keep you hopping.

BASIC BREW (DRIP METHOD)

Coffee lovers everywhere have their own ways of making coffee. Some measure out just enough coffee for the number of cups they plan to make, while others add an extra scoop "for the pot." To find your ideal brew, experiment a bit.

To get you started, here's the *Little Black Book of Coffee's* Rule of (Brown) Thumb Number 1:

For each serving of brewed coffee, use:

- *1 to 2 tablespoons (1 scoop) ground coffee and*
- *3/4 cup to 1 cup (6 to 8 ounces) water*

You'll note that this rule allows for broad variations. This is because coffee preferences and habits vary widely. Should you use one tablespoon or two? The prevailing wisdom among specialty coffee lovers is that a proper cup requires two tablespoons, but other equally ardent coffee fans opt for one. Our rule of thumb says it all depends on how strong you like your coffee, and whether you plan to drink one cup or more, whether you add a lot of milk, a little, or drink it black, and how coffee affects you. Only you know the answer.

One caveat: Unless you are using a single-serve coffee pod or a small, single-serve coffeemaker or have a small-batch setting on your machine, it's best to make at least 4 cups at a time. A little bit of coffee in a big carafe makes for a weak brew.

Many coffee aficionados insist on using filtered water, contending that tap water can impart off-flavors to a cup of coffee. Since the mineral content of water varies from place to place and can affect the water's taste, filtered water is an option worth considering.

Whatever water you use, it's important that it reach the proper temperature: 195°. This temperature allows for optimum extraction of flavor and aroma from the grounds.

BASIC ESPRESSO

Espresso is Italian for "fast"—which is an ideal description for this strong, Italian-inspired coffee. While drip methods use the force of gravity—water drips through the ground coffee from

above—espresso uses pressure to quickly infuse the water with the coffee.

Technically, espresso refers to the drink's method of preparation. But the term is also applied to the degree to which beans used for espresso have been roasted—that is to say, very dark and almost burned. These are then ground very fine, to a powdery consistency.

Whether you buy it pre-ground or grind it yourself, when you measure your espresso into the machine's brewing basket, tamp it—that is, pack it, but gently. If you pack it too tight, the water won't flow through the espresso grounds properly.

Every espresso machine comes with its own

instructions, and you should follow them, of course, but here's *The Little Black Book of Coffee's* Rule of (Brown) Thumb Number 2: For each serving of espresso, use:

- *2 tablespoons finely ground espresso*
- *1/4 cup (2 ounces) water*

Unlike drip coffee makers, many espresso machines designed for the home user make just 1 or 2 small cups, called shots, at a time. Follow the manufacturer's instructions with regard to the number of servings you can make at once.

Your finished cup of espresso should have a bit of foam floating on the top. This is distinct from any frothed milk you might add later; it's a result of the espresso brewing process, and it's called the *crema*.

There are many variations on the basic espresso formula. Cappuccino (page 60), caffe latté (page 59) and cafe mocha (page 61) are among the best known, but there are others, and you'll enjoy learning their Italian names as much as you'll like drinking them. Here are a few.

ESPRESSO SOLO: a single shot of espresso

ESPRESSO DOPPIO: a double espresso, made with twice the amount of espresso and water as a solo

ESPRESSO MACCHIATO: a "marked" espresso, with just a spoonful of steamed milk foam floating on the surface

ESPRESSO RISTRETTO: a "restricted" espresso, made with the same amount of espresso as the espresso solo, but less water

ESPRESSO CON PANNA: an espresso topped with whipped cream

AMERICANO: a solo espresso with as much as a cup of hot water added

LATTE MACCHIATO: a "marked" latte—a cup of steamed milk marked with a shot or less of espresso

LATTE BREVE: a latte made with half and half instead of milk

CAFFE LATTE

Caffe latte is espresso with steamed—not frothed—milk. True latte contains two-thirds milk to one-third espresso. Use a steaming pitcher large enough to allow the milk to expand.

2 tablespoons finely ground espresso
1/4 cup water
1 cup milk
Sweetener to taste, optional

Gently pack espresso into the machine's brew basket. Add water to the water chamber and follow the manufacturer's instructions. Pour espresso into a mug. Pour milk into a stainless steel pitcher, filling it no more than halfway. Insert the steaming nozzle into the bottom of the pitcher and steam milk. Pour steamed milk into espresso. If you wish, stir in sweetener.

1 SERVING

CAPPUCCINO

Cappuccino is espresso dressed with both steamed and frothed milk.

2 tablespoons finely ground espresso
1/4 cup water
1 cup milk
Sweetener to taste, optional

Gently pack espresso into the machine's brew basket. Add water to the water chamber and follow the manufacturer's instructions. Pour espresso into a mug. Pour milk into a stainless steel pitcher, filling it no more than halfway. Insert the steaming nozzle just below the surface and steam and froth milk. Adjust the pitcher as milk volume rises, to keep the nozzle just below the surface. Holding back froth with a spoon, pour steamed milk into espresso. If you wish, stir in sweetener. Then spoon froth into the mug.

1 SERVING

CAFÉ MOCHA

Treat yourself to a cup of comfort.

2 tablespoons finely ground espresso
1/4 cup water
1 tablespoon chocolate syrup
1 cup milk
Sweetener and/or cocoa powder to taste

Gently pack espresso into the machine's brew basket. Add water to the water chamber and follow the manufacturer's brewing instructions. Pour espresso into a mug and stir in chocolate syrup. Pour milk into a stainless steel pitcher, filling it no more than halfway. Insert the steaming nozzle and steam. If you have frothed milk, hold it back in the pitcher with a spoon and pour steamed milk into the mug. If you wish, stir in sweetener, spoon froth on top and sprinkle cocoa powder on the surface.

1 SERVING

ETHIOPIAN-STYLE
SPICED COFFEE

 Early coffee drinkers of Ethiopia, as well as their neighbors in Yemen and elsewhere in the Muslim world, perfumed their coffee with spices such as cinnamon and cardamom. Cardamom can be intense; its strength will depend on its age. Experiment a bit to find out how much you like. Use an automatic drip coffeemaker for this coffee.

4 to 8 tablespoons (2 to 4 scoops) ground
coffee
1/4 to 1/2 teaspoon ground cinnamon
4 to 10 green cardamom pods, gently crushed
4 cups water
Sweetener to taste, optional
Milk or cream to taste, optional

Measure coffee into the filter basket. Add

cinnamon and cardamom seeds and hulls and stir gently. Add water to the water chamber and follow the manufacturer's brewing instructions. Divide coffee equally among 4 mugs. If you wish, add milk or cream and sweetener.

4 SERVINGS

ORANGE-SCENTED COFFEE

 Orange zest gives coffee a heavenly scent. Wash the oranges well and use a vegetable peeler to remove the zest. Peel off the thin outer orange layer only—not the bitter white pith. Don't bother to zest the orange neatly, as the zest will be discarded. When you're done, wash the coffeepot well to rid it of the orange scent and prepare it for your next coffee adventure. Use an automatic drip coffeemaker for this brew.

4 to 8 tablespoons (2 to 4 scoops) ground coffee
4 cups water
Zest of 2 oranges
Sweetener to taste, optional
Milk or cream to taste, optional

Measure coffee into the coffeemaker's filter basket. Add water to the water chamber. Place orange zest into the carafe so that it will steep in coffee as the liquid drips in. Follow the manufacturer's brewing instructions. Strain coffee into 4 mugs. Discard zest. If you wish, add milk and sweetener to each. (If you do not serve the whole pot immediately, strain out the zest anyway; if it steeps for too long, it can make the coffee bitter.)

4 SERVINGS

Café Dulce de Leche

Popular in Argentina and other Latin American countries, *dulce de leche* is a sweet condiment made of caramelized milk. Caramel-brown in color, it has a consistency somewhat similar to peanut butter. Typically used with desserts, breads, and pancakes, it gives coffee a pleasingly sweet, caramel flavor. It is increasingly available in specialty shops, Hispanic groceries, and some supermarkets.

2 cups hot brewed coffee
2 tablespoons dulce de leche, *or to taste*
Milk or cream to taste, optional

Divide coffee evenly between 2 mugs. Add 1 tablespoon *dulce de leche* to each and stir until it is melted and completely dissolved. If you wish, add milk or cream to cool the hot coffee.

2 SERVINGS

CHOCOLATE-HAZELNUT COFFEE

Chocolate and hazelnut give this coffee an Italian accent.

2 cups hot brewed coffee
4 tablespoons hazelnut syrup
3 tablespoons chocolate-hazelnut spread such as Nutella, or to taste
Milk or cream to taste, optional
Sweetener to taste, optional

Divide coffee evenly between 2 mugs. Add 2 tablespoons hazelnut syrup and 1-1/2 tablespoons chocolate-hazelnut spread to each and stir and mash until spread is melted and completely dissolved. (This might take a few minutes. Scrape the bottom and sides of the mug with a spoon to thoroughly blend spread into coffee.) If you wish, add milk or cream and sweetener to taste.

2 SERVINGS

Café Coco

Crema de coco is a canned sweetened coconut cream that's available in the Latin American and/or baking section of many supermarkets. Don't confuse it with the unsweetened canned coconut milk or canned coconut cream that's found in the Asian aisle. It's a different product.

2 cups hot brewed coffee
1/2 cup canned sweetened crema de coco
  (cream of coconut), stirred well before
  measuring

Divide coffee evenly between 2 mugs. Stir *crema de coco* well before measuring it. Add 1/4 cup *crema de coco* to each and stir well.

2 SERVINGS

VANILLA-NUT COFFEE

Vanilla syrup gives you the heavenly flavor and fragrance of vanilla.

2 cups hot brewed coffee
2 tablespoons vanilla syrup
2 teaspoons brown sugar
1 teaspoon almond extract
Milk or cream to taste, optional
Real Whipped Cream to taste, page 160,
  optional
4 pecan halves for garnish, optional

Divide coffee evenly between 2 mugs. Add 1 tablespoon vanilla syrup, 1 teaspoon brown sugar, and 1/2 teaspoon almond extract to each. Stir until all ingredients are well blended and sugar is dissolved. If you wish, add milk or cream to taste, spoon a dollop of whipped cream on top and place 2 pecan halves on top of each.

2 SERVINGS

INSTANT LATTE

This might not technically qualify as a latte, but what it lacks in finesse, it makes up in speed and ease.

1 tablespoon plus 1 teaspoon instant espresso powder, or to taste
2 tablespoons granulated sugar, or to taste
2 pinches salt
2 cups milk

Divide espresso powder, sugar, and salt evenly between 2 mugs. Add 1 tablespoon milk to each and stir until espresso and sugar are completely dissolved and mixture has the consistency of a paste. Pour remaining milk into a microwave-safe container and microwave on high power for 1 to 2 minutes or until it starts to bubble. (Do not boil.) Immediately divide milk between the mugs.

2 SERVINGS

cold coffee drinks

Coffee! Coffee! I must have it.
If I do not have coffee I will die!

<small>FROM BACH'S COFFEE CANTATA</small>

VIETNAMESE ICED COFFEE

Canned condensed milk doesn't spoil in tropical climates like Vietnam's—and it makes an incredibly delicious iced coffee, too. Traditionally, this coffee is brewed in a drip filter that sits atop the glass.

6 tablespoons sweetened condensed milk
Ice cubes
2 cups hot brewed coffee or coffee and hot water to make drip-filtered coffee

Divide condensed milk between 2 tall chilled glasses, pouring it into the center of the glass so it does not stick to the sides. Add enough ice cubes to fill each glass half full. Add 1 cup coffee to each or place a drip filter with coffee and hot water over each glass. When coffee is ready, stir to dissolve milk.

2 SERVINGS

COFFEE 'N' CREAM FLOAT

1-1/2 cups chilled brewed coffee
1 cup cold milk
4 tablespoons caramel syrup
1-1/2 cups cream soda
2 scoops vanilla ice cream, or to taste

Divide coffee and milk evenly between 2 tall chilled glasses. Add 2 tablespoons caramel syrup to each. Stir to blend. Add half the cream soda to each, and top each with 1 scoop ice cream. Serve immediately.

2 SERVINGS

COFFEE EGG CREAM

The Old New York favorite has no eggs, despite its name, and neither does this caffeinated variation. A traditional egg cream consists of milk, chocolate syrup, and seltzer. This one substitutes coffee syrup for chocolate, or you can use both.

2 cups cold milk
6 tablespoons sweetened coffee syrup
1 rounded tablespoon instant coffee
2 tablespoons chocolate syrup, optional
1/4 to 1/2 cup bubbly seltzer or club soda

Divide milk evenly between 2 tall chilled glasses. Add 3 tablespoons coffee syrup, 1/2 tablespoon instant coffee and, if you wish, 1 tablespoon chocolate syrup to each. Stir until syrup and coffee powder are completely dissolved. Add half the club soda to each. Serve immediately.

2 SERVINGS

COFFEE-ORANGE COOLER

2 cups chilled brewed coffee
2 cups orange sherbet
2 cups vanilla ice cream
Fresh mint sprigs for garnish, optional

Pour coffee into a blender, add sherbet and ice cream, and blend until smooth and frothy. Divide evenly between 2 chilled tall glasses, garnish each with a fresh mint sprig if you wish, and serve immediately.

2 SERVINGS

Coffee Colada

*1 (10-ounce) container frozen piña colada
  concentrate*
1 cup chilled brewed coffee
1 cup half and half or light cream
1 to 2 tablespoons instant espresso powder
Pinch of salt

Spoon piña colada concentrate into a
blender. Add coffee, half and half, espresso
powder, and salt, and blend until smooth
and frothy. Divide evenly between 2 chilled
tall glasses and serve immediately.

2 SERVINGS

MEXICAN-SPICED
COFFEE SMOOTHIE

2 teaspoons chili powder, or to taste
1 teaspoon cocoa powder
1 teaspoon ground cinnamon
2 tablespoons brown or granulated sugar, or
  to taste
2 cups chilled brewed coffee
1 cup light cream
About 8 ice cubes

Combine chili and cocoa powders, cinnamon, and sugar in a bowl. Pour mixture into coffee and stir until powders are completely dissolved. Pour into the blender, add cream and ice cubes and blend until smooth and frothy. Taste, add more sugar if necessary, and blend for a few seconds longer. Divide evenly between 2 chilled tall glasses and serve immediately.

2 SERVINGS

RASPBERRY COFFEE SMOOTHIE

*About 1 cup frozen raspberries (about 60
    berries)*
1 cup half and half or light cream, divided
1/4 cup grenadine
2 cups chilled brewed coffee
2 tablespoons confectioners' sugar, or to taste
8 ice cubes
1 teaspoon instant espresso powder, optional

 Pour raspberries and 1/2 cup cream into the blender and blend until smooth. Strain through a fine-mesh sieve to remove seeds, mashing to get as much raspberry pulp as you can. Rinse the blender and all parts thoroughly and return raspberries to it. Add remaining cream and other ingredients except espresso powder and blend until smooth and frothy. Taste, and add espresso powder if desired, and more sugar if necessary, blending

for a few seconds longer. Divide evenly between 2 chilled tall glasses and serve.

2 SERVINGS

JAVA JOLT SMOOTHIE

1 cup chilled brewed coffee
1 banana, peeled, sliced, and frozen
3/4 cup nonfat vanilla frozen yogurt
1/4 teaspoon ground cinnamon

Pour coffee into a blender. Add banana slices, frozen yogurt, and cinnamon. Blend until smooth and frothy. Pour into 2 tall chilled glasses and serve immediately.

2 SERVINGS

COFFEE-MAPLE WHIP

2 cups chilled brewed coffee
1 cup half and half or light cream
1/4 cup pure maple syrup, or to taste
6 to 8 ice cubes
Real Whipped Cream to taste, page 160,
   optional
4 walnut halves for garnish, optional

Pour coffee, half and half, and maple syrup
into a blender, add ice, and blend until
smooth and frothy. Taste and add more
maple syrup if necessary and blend for a few
seconds longer. Divide evenly between 2
chilled tall glasses. If you wish, spoon a dollop of whipped cream on top of each and
float 2 walnut halves on the
surface of each drink for garnish. Serve immediately.

2 SERVINGS

Hazelnut-Espresso Granita

Many recipes tell you to make granita by putting your ingredients into a baking pan, putting the pan in the freezer and stirring it every 20 minutes, so it will get properly slushy. Here's the easy way: freeze the ingredient mixture in ice cube trays and use the food processor to transform it to slush.

2-1/2 cups water, divided
2 teaspoons instant espresso powder
2 teaspoons hazelnut or other flavored syrup, or to taste, optional
2 teaspoons confectioners' sugar, or to taste, optional
1/4 cup chilled brewed coffee
1/4 cup granulated sugar
Fresh mint sprigs for garnish, optional

Mix 2 cups water, espresso powder, hazelnut

syrup, and confectioners' sugar until espresso and sugar are completely dissolved. Carefully pour into 2 standard ice cube trays. Freeze overnight.

When you are ready to make the granita, remove the trays from the freezer and transfer the espresso cubes into a food processor fitted with a metal blade. Add remaining 1/2 cup water, brewed coffee, and granulated sugar. Process until smooth and slushy. Stop the machine periodically to scrape down the sides of the processor bowl with a rubber spatula and loosen any cubes that are stuck to the blade. Divide evenly between 2 chilled tall glasses. If you wish, garnish with fresh mint sprigs. Serve immediately.

2 SERVINGS

ESPRESSO BOOST SMOOTHIE

1/2 cup chilled espresso
1/2 cup chilled nonfat milk
1 banana, peeled, sliced, and frozen
3/4 cup chocolate sorbet
3 ice cubes, crushed

Pour espresso and milk into a blender and add banana slices, sorbet, and crushed ice. Blend at high speed until smooth and frothy. Pour into 2 tall chilled glasses and serve immediately.

2 SERVINGS

spirited coffee drinks

Home on the range; the break of day, the chuck-wagon, the surly, sleepy cowboys, the coffeepot pushed up against the fire. . . . you've never in your life wondered what variety of coffee boils in that vary basic pot. It just has to be good . . . which is to say, strong, hot and tasting like coffee.

JOHN THRONE

IRISH COFFEE

3 ounces Irish whiskey
1-1/2 cups hot brewed coffee
2 teaspoons brown sugar
Heavy cream or Real Whipped Cream to
*   taste, page 160*
Ground cinnamon to taste, optional
Cocoa powder to taste, optional
2 cinnamon sticks

Warm 2 heatproof Irish coffee glasses or coffee mugs by filling them with very hot water for a few minutes. Drain and dry well. Divide Irish whiskey, coffee and brown sugar evenly between the mugs and stir to combine. Gently pour or spoon the cream into each, so that it floats on the surface of the drink. Do not mix. If you wish, sprinkle with cinnamon or cocoa powder. Use cinnamon sticks for stirrers.

2 SERVINGS

IRISH MIST COFFEE

1-1/2 ounces Irish whiskey
1-1/2 ounces Irish Mist liqueur
1-1/2 cups hot brewed coffee
2 teaspoons brown sugar
Real Whipped Cream to taste, page 160
Ground cinnamon to taste, optional
Cocoa powder to taste, optional

Warm 2 heatproof Irish coffee glasses or coffee mugs by filling them with very hot water for a few minutes. Drain and dry well. Divide Irish whiskey, Irish Mist, coffee, and brown sugar equally between the mugs and stir to combine. Spoon whipped cream on the surface of each. If you wish, sprinkle with cinnamon or cocoa powder.

2 SERVINGS

NUTTY IRISH COFFEE

1-1/2 ounces Irish whiskey
1-1/2 ounces Frangelico liqueur
1-1/2 cups hot brewed coffee
2 teaspoons brown sugar
Real Whipped Cream to taste, page 160
Ground cinnamon to taste, optional
Cocoa powder to taste, optional

Warm 2 heatproof Irish coffee glasses or coffee mugs by filling them with very hot water for a few minutes. Drain and dry well. Divide Irish whiskey, Frangelico, coffee, and brown sugar equally between the mugs and stir to combine. Spoon whipped cream on the surface of each. If you wish, sprinkle with cinnamon or cocoa powder.

2 SERVINGS

MEXICAN COFFEE

2 ounces coffee flavored liqueur
1 ounce tequila
1-1/2 cups hot brewed coffee
Sweetener to taste, optional
Real Whipped Cream to taste, page 160

Warm 2 coffee glasses or coffee mugs by filling them with very hot water for a few minutes. Drain and dry well. Divide liqueur and tequila evenly between the mugs. Add half the coffee to each and, if you wish, the sweetener of your choice, to taste. Stir to combine. Spoon whipped cream on the surface of each.

2 SERVINGS

SPANISH COFFEE

The mixologist named this bracing cup Spanish coffee, doubtless because of the Spanish name of one of its principal ingredients. But Tía Maria is actually a Jamaican liqueur flavored with Blue Mountain coffee, rum, and spices.

1-1/2 ounces Irish whiskey
1-1/2 ounces Tía Maria liqueur
1-1/2 cups hot brewed coffee
2 teaspoons brown sugar
Real Whipped Cream to taste, page 160
Ground cinnamon to taste, optional
Cocoa powder to taste, optional
Espresso beans, for garnish, optional

Warm 2 coffee mugs by filling them with very hot water for a few minutes. Drain and dry well. Divide Irish whiskey, Tía Maria, coffee, and brown sugar equally between the mugs and stir to combine. Spoon whipped cream on the surface of each. If you wish, sprinkle with cinnamon or cocoa powder and float a few espresso beans in each cup.

2 SERVINGS

JAMAICAN COFFEE

2 ounces coffee-flavored liqueur
2 ounces Jamaican rum
1-1/2 cups hot brewed coffee
Sweetener to taste, optional
Real Whipped Cream to taste, page 160
Pinch of ground allspice, optional

Warm 2 coffee mugs by filling them with very hot water for a few minutes. Drain and dry well. Divide coffee liqueur and rum evenly between the mugs. Add half the coffee to each and, if you wish, the sweetener of your choice, to taste. Stir to combine. Spoon whipped cream on the surface of each. If you wish, sprinkle with allspice.

2 SERVINGS

CAFFE AMARETTO

3 ounces amaretto liqueur
1-1/2 cups hot brewed coffee
Real Whipped Cream to taste, page 160

Warm 2 coffee mugs by filling them with very hot water for a few minutes. Drain and dry well. Divide the amaretto and coffee evenly between the mugs. Stir. Spoon whipped cream on the surface of each.

2 SERVINGS

CHOCOLATE ALMOND COFFEE

1-1/2 ounces amaretto
1 ounce crème de cacao
1-1/2 cups hot brewed coffee
Heavy cream to taste
Chocolate shavings, for garnish

Warm 2 coffee mugs by filling them with very hot water for a few minutes. Drain and dry well. Divide amaretto, crème de cacao, and coffee evenly between the mugs and stir to combine. Pour cream in gently so it floats on the surface of the drinks. Do not mix. Garnish each with chocolate shavings.

2 SERVINGS

FLAMING CAFÉ ROYALE

2 sugar cubes
1 ounce brandy
2 cups hot brewed coffee
2 tablespoons heavy cream, optional

Soak sugar cubes in brandy. Warm 2 coffee mugs with very hot water for a few minutes. Drain and dry well. Divide coffee between the mugs. Rest a teaspoon across the top of each mug, so the concave side sits above the coffee, facing up.

Place 1 cube into each spoon and carefully divide brandy between the spoons. Let stand for a few minutes; then carefully ignite both brandy-filled spoons with a long match. Let the flames burn out. Stir sugar and brandy into coffees. If you wish, gently pour 1 tablespoon cream into each, so it floats on surface of drink. Do not mix.

2 SERVINGS

CHILLED MOCHA WAKE-UP

A special drink for Sunday brunch on a hot summer day.

2 cups nonfat or 1 percent milk
1 cup cold brewed coffee
1 cup chocolate syrup
1/2 cup crème de cacao
1 teaspoon ground cinnamon

Pour milk, coffee, chocolate syrup, and crème de cacao into a blender and add the cinnamon. Blend at high speed until frothy. Pour into 4 chilled tall glasses and serve immediately.

4 SERVINGS

B-52

This potent cocktail is known as a pousse café, in which the various ingredients float one on top of the other. It's ideally served in a pousse café glass, a slender cocktail glass with a stem, which holds about an ounce. If you don't have pousse café glasses, substitute slender champagne flutes.

2/3 ounce coffee-flavored liqueur
2/3 ounce Irish cream liqueur
2/3 ounce Grand Marnier

Place spoons into 2 pousse café glasses, round side up, and pour 1/3 ounce coffee liqueur over each. Change spoons and repeat with Irish cream liqueur, but don't allow the spoon to touch the liquid already in the glass. Change spoons again and repeat with Grand Marnier. Serve immediately.

2 SERVINGS

ESPRESSO MARTINI

Cracked ice
3 ounces vodka or vanilla-flavored vodka
1 ounce coffee-flavored liqueur
4 to 6 espresso beans, optional, for garnish

Fill a cocktail shaker with cracked ice. Add vodka and coffee liqueur. Stir to blend and strain into 2 chilled martini glasses. If you wish, garnish each with 2 or 3 espresso beans and serve.

2 SERVINGS

MIDNIGHT MARTINI

Cracked ice
3 ounces vodka
1/2 ounce coffee-flavored liqueur
1/2 ounce triple sec or orange liqueur
2 orange slices, for garnish

Fill a cocktail shaker with cracked ice. Add vodka, coffee liqueur, and triple sec. Stir to blend and strain into 2 chilled martini glasses. Garnish each with an orange slice and serve.

2 SERVINGS

CLASSIC BLACK (OR WHITE) RUSSIAN

The addition of cream transforms the Black Russian into its white (actually beige) cousin. Either way, it's good. Serve it neat or on the rocks.

Cracked ice
4 ounces vodka
2 ounces coffee-flavored liqueur
2 tablespoons heavy cream, optional
Ice cubes, optional

Fill a cocktail shaker with cracked ice. Add vodka, coffee liqueur and, if desired, cream. Shake well. If you wish to serve on the rocks, place ice cubes into 2 chilled old-fashioned glasses. Strain mixture into the glasses and serve immediately.

2 SERVINGS

MUDSLIDE

Cracked ice
1-1/2 ounces vodka
1-1/2 ounces coffee-flavored liqueur
1-1/2 ounces Irish cream liqueur
Chocolate curls, optional, for garnish

Fill a cocktail shaker with cracked ice. Add vodka and liqueurs. Stir to blend and strain into 2 chilled cocktail glasses. If you wish, garnish each with chocolate curls and serve.

2 SERVINGS

CAFÉ ROMANO

When in Rome . . . or anywhere.

Cracked ice
2 ounces sambuca
2 ounces coffee-flavored liqueur
1/4 cup heavy cream

Fill a cocktail shaker with cracked ice. Add

Fill a cocktail shaker with cracked ice. Add sambuca, coffee liqueur, and cream. Shake well. Strain into 2 chilled cocktail glasses and serve.

2 SERVINGS

PEPPERMINT PATTY

Cracked ice
1 ounce coffee-flavored liqueur
1 ounce peppermint schnapps
2 tablespoons heavy cream

Fill a cocktail shaker with cracked ice. Add coffee liqueur, schnapps, and cream. Shake well. Strain into 2 chilled shot glasses and serve immediately.

2 SERVINGS

COFFEE GRASSHOPPER

The original Grasshopper is a triple-cream concoction of crème de cacao, crème de menthe, and cream. The coffee version substitutes coffee-flavored liqueur for crème de cacao, with delicious results.

Cracked ice
2 ounces coffee-flavored liqueur
2 ounces crème de menthe
1/4 cup heavy cream
Ice cubes, optional

Fill a shaker with cracked ice. Pour coffee liqueur, crème de menthe, and cream into it and shake well. If you wish, add ice cubes to 2 chilled old-fashioned glasses, Strain mixture into the glasses and serve immediately.

2 SERVINGS

treats made with coffee

Good coffee should be black like the devil,

hot like hell, and sweet like a kiss.

HUNGARIAN SAYING

MOCHA CHEESECAKE

Chocolate Crumb Pie Crust, page 159

8 squares (1 ounce each) semisweet chocolate

1 tablespoon instant coffee

3 tablespoons boiling water

3 packages (8 ounces each) cream cheese, softened

3/4 cup granulated sugar

3 eggs

3 tablespoons all-purpose flour

1 cup heavy cream

1 teaspoon pure vanilla extract or almond extract

Real Whipped Cream to taste, page 160, optional, for garnish

Preheat oven to 350°. Prepare Chocolate Crumb Pie Crust in a springform pan.

To prepare filling, melt chocolate in a saucepan over medium heat. Remove from the heat and set aside to cool. Dissolve coffee in boiling water and set aside to cool. Place cream cheese in a mixing  bowl and add sugar. With an electric mixer set at medium speed, mix until light and fluffy. Add eggs, 1 at a time, mixing well after each addition and stopping the mixer to scrape the bowl and beaters as needed. Add flour and mix until thoroughly blended. Stir in melted chocolate and coffee. Add cream and vanilla and mix 3 minutes longer, or until well combined.

Pour filling into cooled crust and bake 1 hour. Then turn off oven, keeping the door closed, and leave cake inside for 1 hour longer. Remove cake from oven and cool completely on a wire rack. Cover and refrigerate until ready to serve.

To serve, run a knife around edge of cake and remove the side of the springform pan. If you wish, garnish with swirls of whipped cream.

12 TO 18 SERVINGS

JAVA BALLS

1 box (12 ounces) vanilla wafers, crushed
1/2 cup cocoa powder, plus more for dusting
3/4 cup confectioners' sugar
3/4 cup chopped walnuts, optional
1/4 cup light corn syrup
4 ounces coffee-flavored liqueur
1 to 2 tablespoons cold espresso

Combine vanilla wafers, cocoa powder, confectioners' sugar, and nuts, if using, in a large bowl. Add corn syrup, coffee liqueur and espresso, and mix well; the mixture should be just moist enough to form into balls without sticking to your hands. Dust your hands lightly with cocoa powder and form the mixture into balls. Roll balls in cocoa powder. Transfer to an airtight container and refrigerate for 2 to 3 days before serving. Dust with more cocoa powder if needed.

ABOUT 36 BALLS

CHOCOLATE SOUFFLÉ

Nonstick vegetable oil spray or vegetable oil
for greasing
1/3 cup sifted cornstarch, plus more for
dusting
3 tablespoons instant coffee
3 tablespoons boiling water
6 squares (1-ounce each) semisweet chocolate,
chopped
1-1/2 cups milk
1/2 cup plus 2 tablespoons granulated sugar
5 eggs, separated, plus whites of 2 eggs
1/4 teaspoon cream of tartar
Pinch of salt

Preheat oven to 375°. Spray or grease a 2-1/2-quart soufflé dish and dust it with a little cornstarch. Tap out any excess. Cut a piece of aluminum foil about 1-1/2 inches longer than the circumference of the soufflé dish. Fold foil in half lengthwise and spray or grease 1 side. Wrap foil around the soufflé

dish, with greased side in, to extend the height of the dish.

Pour coffee into a small, heavy saucepan and stir in 3 tablespoons boiling water. Stir to dissolve. Add chocolate and cook over low heat until melted. Set aside to cool.

Pour 1/3 cup sifted cornstarch into a large saucepan and stir in a few tablespoons of milk, stirring vigorously until completely smooth. Stir in remaining milk and 1/2 cup sugar. Cook over medium heat, stirring constantly, until the mixture comes to a boil and thickens. Spoon into a large bowl and beat in chocolate mixture. Add 5 egg yolks and beat to incorporate.

Using an electric mixer set at medium speed, beat 7 egg whites in a mixing bowl, until frothy. Add cream of tartar and salt and beat to soft peaks. Add remaining 2 tablespoons sugar and beat until stiff peaks form.

Fold into chocolate mixture.

Bake for about 55 minutes; do not open oven door while baking. Serve immediately.

6 TO 8 SERVINGS

COLD MOCHA SOUFFLÉ

1-1/2 envelopes (1-1/2 tablespoons)
* unflavored powdered gelatin*
3 tablespoons cold water
6 squares (1-ounce each) unsweetened
* chocolate*
3/4 cup confectioners' sugar
3/4 strong brewed coffee
3/4 cup milk
1-1/4 cups granulated sugar
2 tablespoons crème de cacao
Pinch of salt
3 cups heavy cream

Dissolve gelatin in cold water and set aside.
Melt chocolate in a saucepan over low heat,
stirring and being careful that it doesn't burn.
Remove from the heat, add confectioners'
sugar, and stir until smooth.

In a separate saucepan, heat coffee and milk over medium heat
just until bubbles begin to form

around the edges. Pour into chocolate mixture slowly, stirring constantly until mixture is smooth and well combined.

Set mixture over medium heat, and cook, stirring constantly, just until it comes to a simmer. (Do not boil.) Immediately remove from the heat and stir in softened gelatin, granulated sugar, crème de cacao, and salt. Spoon into a large mixing bowl, cover with plastic wrap and refrigerate until moderately thickened.

Meanwhile, in a separate bowl, beat cream until thickened and soft peaks form.

When chocolate mixture is thickened, remove from the refrigerator and beat until light and airy. Fold in whipped cream and spoon into serving bowl. Refrigerate for at least 2-1/2 hours. Serve cold.

10 SERVINGS

DESSERT CREPES WITH BUTTER PECAN ICE CREAM AND MOCHA GLAZE

Crepe batter needs to rest for at least 20 minutes so the flour can fully absorb the liquid. Vary the ice cream flavor if you like.

1 cup all-purpose flour
1 teaspoon granulated sugar
1 cup whole milk
3 eggs
1/3 cup water
3 tablespoons unsalted butter, melted
Mocha Glaze, page 128, or bottled coffee or
    mocha syrup
Vegetable oil and melted butter for frying
Butter pecan ice cream
Fresh mint sprigs for garnish

To prepare crepe batter, pour flour, sugar, milk, eggs, water, and melted butter into a blender or food processor fitted with a metal blade and process until smooth. (Or beat with a fork until smooth.) Cover and set aside for at least 20 minutes, or make the batter in advance and refrigerate it for several hours or overnight.

Meanwhile, prepare Mocha Glaze.

When you are ready to cook crepes, heat a crepe pan or small frying pan over high heat. Mix a few tablespoons oil and melted butter in a heatproof container. Pour mixture into the pan, swirl to coat the surface, and pour any excess back into the heatproof container. (The pan should be just lightly coated.)

With a ladle or coffee scoop, pour about 2 tablespoons batter into the pan and tilt the pan from side to side so that batter spreads to form a very thin, round crepe. Heat for 30 to 45 seconds, until tiny bubbles form in crepe and underside is golden brown. Turn crepe with a spatula and cook for 15 to 20 seconds. The second side will not be as brown as the first. Remove from the heat and place on a platter. Repeat the process with remaining batter, separating finished crepes with waxed paper. (You should have at least 12 crepes.)

To assemble, place 2 crepes (side by side) on each plate, scoop some ice cream into the center of each, and roll each lightly. Drizzle Mocha Glaze over each plate, garnish with mint sprigs, and serve.

12 CREPES (6 SERVINGS)

MINIATURE MOCHA CUPCAKES

1/2 cup chocolate morsels
1/2 cup (1 stick) unsalted butter
3/4 cup granulated sugar
1/2 cup all-purpose flour
1 teaspoon instant espresso powder
2 tablespoons hot water
2 eggs, beaten
1/2 cup finely chopped walnuts or pecans
24 walnut or pecan halves

Preheat oven to 350°. Line 24 miniature (1-1/2-inch) muffin cups with paper liners. Place chocolate morsels and butter in a medium-size heavy saucepan and cook over low heat until melted. Remove from heat and set aside to cool slightly.

Combine sugar and flour in a bowl and stir. Set aside.

Dissolve espresso powder in 2 tablespoons hot water and set aside.

Add beaten eggs to chocolate mixture, beating until well combined. Stir in flour mixture, espresso, and chopped nuts. Spoon batter into prepared muffin cups, filling them 2/3 full. Top each cupcake with a walnut or pecan half and bake for 18 to 20 minutes. Cool in the pan for 5 minutes. Remove cupcakes from the pan and transfer to wire racks to cool completely.

24 MINIATURE CUPCAKES

Chocolate Roll

*Butter or nonstick vegetable oil spray for
  greasing*
5 large eggs, separated
2/3 cup granulated sugar
6 (1-ounce each) semisweet chocolate squares
3 tablespoons strong brewed coffee
Cocoa powder
*2 to 2-1/2 cups Real Whipped Cream,
  page 160, divided*
Chocolate shavings, for garnish

Grease a 12-by-8-inch baking sheet, line it
with parchment paper, and grease the paper.
Preheat the oven to 350°.

Beat egg yolks and sugar in a large mixing
bowl until thickened and pale yellow in color.

Combine chocolate and coffee
in a saucepan and set over low
heat, stirring until chocolate is
melted. Remove from the heat

 and let cool. Stir into egg yolk mixture.

Using an electric mixer set at medium speed, beat egg whites in a separate mixing bowl until stiff peaks form. Fold them into egg yolk mixture.

Spread mixture on the prepared baking sheet and smooth to an even thickness. Bake for 15 minutes, or until a toothpick inserted into the center comes out clean. Do not overbake.

Remove the baking sheet from the oven and cover with a damp cloth. Let stand for 30 minutes, or until cool. When cool, loosen cake from baking sheet and dust it generously with cocoa powder. Place a sheet of waxed paper over it to cover it completely. With one hand on each end, grasp the baking sheet and waxed paper and carefully invert the cake onto the paper, cocoa side down. Remove parchment paper.

Prepare a serving plate and set it next to the cake. Spread cake evenly with whipped cream, reserving about 3/4 cup. Roll up like a jellyroll, using the waxed paper to lift and roll cake, and then pulling the paper away from the rolled section as you go. Position the serving plate so that the last roll deposits it onto the plate. Spread remaining whipped cream on top. Garnish with chocolate shavings.

8 SERVINGS

COFFEE LOVER'S TIRAMISU

 There's a reason why tiramisu is a perennial after-dinner favorite. It's delicious! Many recipes add whipped egg whites to the mascarpone topping for extra lightness. Pasteurized liquid egg white (found in the dairy aisle) achieves the same goal but avoids the risk of foodborne illness that comes with raw eggs.

1/2 cup pasteurized liquid egg white product
6 ounces coffee liqueur, or 3 ounces coffee
   liqueur and 3 ounces chocolate liqueur
3/4 cup cold brewed coffee
16 lady fingers
1 pound mascarpone cheese
1/3 cup confectioners' sugar
3 to 4 ounces dark chocolate, shaved or
   grated, for garnish
Chocolate-covered espresso beans, and/or

strawberries for garnish, optional

Whisk egg white product until light in color and soft peaks form. If you wish, use a food processor, but be careful not to overmix.

Combine liqueur(s) and coffee in a shallow bowl. Dip lady fingers into mixture, place 4 lady fingers each onto 4 serving dishes, and set aside. Reserve remaining coffee mixture.

Spoon mascarpone into a medium mixing bowl and add sugar and remaining coffee mixture. Mix until thoroughly combined. Fold egg white into mascarpone mixture and mix gently until thoroughly combined. Spoon a generous amount of topping over lady fingers in each dish. Sprinkle with chocolate shavings. Garnish each dish with espresso beans and/or 1 or 2 strawberries, if desired.

4 SERVINGS

ICE CREAM WITH MOCHA SABAYON

Coffee-flavored liqueur substitutes for the usual Marsala wine or sherry used in traditional sabayon recipes. Measure all your ingredients in advance and have them handy, as this tasty treat cooks quickly.

6 egg yolks
1/4 cup confectioners' sugar
3 tablespoons unsweetened cocoa powder
1 teaspoon instant espresso powder
1/4 cup coffee-flavored liqueur
4 scoops vanilla ice cream

Fill the bottom of a double boiler partway up

 with water and test to make sure water does not touch the top of the double boiler when you set it on. Set the bottom pan over low heat and bring to a simmer. Do not boil.

Meanwhile, in the top part, beat egg yolks lightly. Add confectioners' sugar, cocoa and espresso powders, and coffee liqueur. Place over the simmering water and stir constantly until mixture is smooth, has nearly doubled in volume, and an inserted thermometer reads 160°. Scrape the sides of the double boiler with a rubber spatula to incorporate all ingredients. If mixture cooks too quickly, remove the top of the double boiler from the heat and stir briskly; return to the heat and continue cooking. Remove from the heat. (If sabayon cooks too much and gets lumpy, strain through a fine-mesh sieve.)

Scoop ice cream into 4 ice cream dishes and spoon sabayon over each. Serve immediately.

4 SERVINGS

MOCHA POTS DE CRÈME

6 egg yolks
2 cups half and half
4 squares (1-ounce each) semisweet chocolate,
* coarsely chopped*
1/4 cup granulated sugar
1/8 teaspoon salt
3 tablespoons coffee-flavored liqueur
Real Whipped Cream, page 160, optional, for
* garnish*

Preheat the oven to 325°. Lightly beat egg yolks in a mixing bowl and set aside.

Pour half and half into small saucepan and set over medium heat until small bubbles begin to form on the sides of the pan. Immediately remove from the heat, add chocolate, and stir until melted. Stir in sugar and salt. Slowly add 3 tablespoons of the chocolate mixture to egg yolks, beating constantly. Then slowly pour egg mixture back into chocolate mixture, beating constantly. Stir in coffee liqueur.

Strain into 6 small heatproof ramekins, custard cups, or individual soufflé dishes. Place filled ramekins in a baking pan and place the pan into the oven. Pour enough hot water into the baking pan to come halfway up the sides of the ramekins. Bake for about 25 minutes or until set. Remove from the oven, cool slightly; then remove ramekins from the baking pan, cover with plastic wrap and refrigerate until chilled. To serve, if you wish, spoon a dollop of whipped cream on each.

6 SERVINGS

CHOCOLATE MALAKOFF

Allow at least 6 hours for this scrumptious dessert to chill.

4 squares (1-ounce each) semisweet chocolate
3/4 cup coffee-flavored liqueur, divided
1/2 cup water
About 24 ladyfinger cookies
1 cup (2 sticks) unsalted butter, softened
1 cup superfine sugar
1-1/3 cups ground almonds (about 6 ounces whole almonds)
2 cups heavy cream
1/4 teaspoon almond extract
Slivered almonds for garnish

Line the sides of a 9-inch springform pan with parchment paper. Melt chocolate and let cool. Pour 1/2 cup coffee liqueur and water into a shallow soup bowl and stir. Dip each ladyfinger into liqueur mixture quickly and stand upright around the side of the prepared springform pan. Set aside. Using an electric mixer set at medium speed, mix butter and sugar until light and creamy. Scrape down the sides of the bowl as necessary with a rubber spatula. Add ground almonds and beat until well combined. Fold in cooled chocolate.

In a separate bowl, with clean beaters and the mixer set at medium speed, mix cream until soft peaks form. Add remaining 1/4 cup coffee liqueur and beat until firm. Fold whipped cream into chocolate mixture and pour into springform pan. Smooth the top, cover lightly with waxed paper and refrigerate for at least 6 hours or overnight.

Shortly before you plan to serve, remove the side of the springform pan, remove the parchment paper and transfer Chocolate Malakoff to a serving plate. If you wish, sprinkle slivered almonds on top.

8 TO 10 SERVINGS

Coffee "Lava" Sundae

8 scoops vanilla ice cream, or to taste
4 tablespoons coffee-flavored liqueur, or to
  taste
2 tablespoons butterscotch sauce, or to taste
2 tablespoons chocolate syrup, or to taste
Chocolate chips to taste
Peanut butter chips to taste

 Scoop equal portions of ice cream into 4 chilled ice cream dishes. Drizzle coffee liqueur over the top of each, holding your measuring spoon over the center of each dish, so that liqueur pours down all sides. In the same fashion, drizzle butterscotch sauce and chocolate syrup over each dish.

Sprinkle with chocolate chips and peanut butter chips.

4 SERVINGS

Coffee Lover's Sundae

There's coffee flavor in every component of this luscious sundae.

Mocha Glaze, page 128
8 scoops coffee ice cream, or to taste
Coffee-flavored liqueur to taste
Chocolate-covered espresso beans

Prepare Mocha Glaze. Scoop equal portions of ice cream into 4 chilled ice cream dishes. Drizzle coffee liqueur over the top of each, holding your measuring cup over the center of each scoop. Drizzle Mocha Glaze over each in the same fashion. Sprinkle with chocolate-covered espresso beans.

4 SERVINGS

MOCHA GLAZE

Use this for crepes, ice cream, and dessert bars.

1 teaspoon instant coffee powder
1/2 cup boiling water
1/3 cup granulated sugar
1 tablespoon vegetable shortening
5 squares (1-ounce each) semisweet chocolate

Dissolve coffee in boiling water. Pour dissolved coffee into a saucepan and stir in sugar and shortening. Bring to a boil; then reduce the heat to low and add chocolate. Cook, stirring, until chocolate is melted. Remove from heat and beat until smooth. Let stand until cool. Stir if necessary just before using.

treats to eat
with coffee

Only one thing is certain about coffee . . . .
Wherever it is grown, sold, brewed, and
consumed, there will be lively controversy,
strong opinions, and good conversation.

MARK PENDERGRAST

BLUEBERRY-APPLE CRISP

Enjoy this fruit crisp for a special breakfast or as the end of a summer picnic. Either way, put on the coffee pot.

Nonstick vegetable oil spray for greasing
3 cups blueberries, washed and drained
3 cups cored, sliced tart apples such as Granny
  Smith, Fuji, or Gala
Brown sugar to taste
1 cup all-purpose flour
3/4 cup granulated sugar
1 teaspoon baking powder
3/4 teaspoon salt
1 egg (not beaten)
1/3 cup unsalted butter, melted and cooled
1/2 teaspoon ground cinnamon
Real Whipped Cream to taste, page 160,
  optional

Preheat the oven to 350°. Grease a baking dish. Add blueberries and apples and stir just to blend. Sprinkle with brown sugar.

Combine flour, sugar, baking powder, salt and egg in a large mixing bowl and mix with a fork until well blended and crumbly. Sprinkle over fruit. Top with melted butter and sprinkle with cinnamon. Bake for 30 minutes or until top is golden brown. Garnish with whipped cream, if you wish, and serve warm.

6 TO 8 SERVINGS

SUGAR COOKIES

To decorate these classic cookies, use colored sugar, available in the supermarket's baking aisle or in specialty baking stores.

1/2 cup (1 stick) unsalted butter, softened
1/2 cup granulated sugar
1 egg
1 tablespoon milk or cream
1/2 teaspoon pure vanilla extract
1/2 teaspoon lemon extract
1-1/2 cups all-purpose flour
1/4 teaspoon salt
Nonstick vegetable oil spray for greasing
Colored sugar for decorating

Combine butter and sugar in a large mixing bowl and mix until creamy. Add egg, milk, and vanilla and lemon extracts, and mix until thoroughly combined. Add flour, a little at a time, and mix to combine. Add salt and mix. Cover the bowl with plastic wrap and refrigerate for about 1 hour.

Preheat oven to 350°. Grease 2 or more baking sheets. Transfer dough to a work surface and roll thinly, to a thickness of 1/16 inch. Use small cookie cutters to cut into shapes. Reroll scraps to cut more cookies. Sprinkle with colored sugar and place on the prepared cookie sheets, working in batches. Bake 1 sheet for 5 to 6 minutes or until golden. Watch carefully to be sure cookies do not brown too much. Cool on the baking sheet for 5 minutes and transfer to wire racks to cool completely. Repeat with remaining dough, rotating your baking sheets.

ABOUT 80 SMALL COOKIES

CITRUS COOKIES

Zest the lemon and then squeeze the juice to give fresh flavor and aroma to these tasty cookies.

1/2 cup (1 stick) unsalted butter softened
1/4 cup granulated sugar
1 egg, separated
1 tablespoon grated orange zest
1 teaspoon grated lemon zest
1 teaspoon fresh lemon juice
1 cup all-purpose flour
1/8 teaspoon salt
Nonstick vegetable oil spray
1/2 cup finely chopped walnuts
10 candied cherries, halved

Mix butter and sugar in a mixing bowl until creamy. Beat egg yolk and add to butter mixture. Add orange and lemon zest and lemon juice. Mix thoroughly. Stir in flour and salt and mix to combine. Cover bowl with plastic and refrigerate until firm.

Preheat oven to 325°. Grease 2 baking sheets. Beat egg white gently in a shallow bowl. Pour chopped nuts into a separate shallow bowl. Transfer dough to a work surface and form into 20 balls, each about 1/2-inch in diameter. Dip balls into egg white and then into nuts. Place on the prepared baking sheets. Press 1/2 candied cherry into the center of each. Bake 1 sheet for 20 minutes. Cool on the baking sheet for about 5 minutes and transfer to wire racks to cool completely. Repeat with remaining sheet.

20 COOKIES

CHOCOLATE WAFERS

1-1/4 cups all-purpose flour, plus more
* for dusting*
1/4 cup unsweetened cocoa powder
1/4 teaspoon baking powder
1/4 teaspoon salt
1/2 cup (1 stick) unsalted butter, softened
1 cup granulated sugar
1 egg
1 teaspoon pure vanilla extract

Preheat oven to 375°. Sift flour, cocoa, baking powder, and salt into a bowl and stir to blend.

In a separate bowl, mix butter and sugar until light and fluffy. Beat in egg and vanilla until thoroughly combined. Using a rubber spatula, fold butter mixture into flour mixture and blend thoroughly. Shape batter into about 24 walnut-sized balls and place on 2 ungreased

baking sheets, about 2 inches apart. Dip a fork into a little flour and tap off any excess. Use fork to press cookies to flatten them. Bake 1 sheet for 8 to 10 minutes. Cool on the baking sheet for about 5 minutes and transfer to wire racks to cool completely. Repeat with remaining sheet.

24 WAFERS

OLD-FASHIONED SOFT COOKIES

Nonstick vegetable oil spray for greasing
2 cups sifted all-purpose flour
1/2 teaspoon baking soda
1/2 teaspoon salt
1/2 cup (1 stick) unsalted butter, softened
1 cup granulated sugar
1 egg, separated
1/2 teaspoon pure vanilla extract
1/2 cup buttermilk

Preheat the oven to 350°. Grease 2 baking sheets. Sift flour, baking soda, and salt into a mixing bowl and stir to blend. In a separate large mixing bowl, mix butter and sugar until

 creamy. Add the egg yolk and mix until fluffy. Add vanilla and mix well.

Add 1/3 of flour mixture to butter mixture and mix to

combine. Add 1/3 of buttermilk and mix to combine. Repeat with remaining flour mixture and buttermilk, 1/3 at a time.

In a separate bowl, beat egg white until stiff. Using a rubber spatula, fold it into batter. Drop by tablespoons, 3 inches apart, onto the prepared baking sheets, to make 18 cookies. Flatten with a spatula to 1/2-inch thickness. Bake 1 sheet for 15 minutes, or until golden brown. Cool on the baking sheet for about 5 minutes and transfer to wire racks to cool completely. Repeat with remaining sheet.

18 COOKIES

CINNAMON NUT SQUARES

1 cup (2 sticks) unsalted butter, softened
1 cup brown sugar
1 egg, separated
2 cups all-purpose flour
1 teaspoon ground cinnamon
1/2 teaspoon salt
1/3 cup chopped pecans

Preheat the oven to 250°. Mix butter and brown sugar in a mixing bowl until creamy. Add egg yolk and mix until combined. Sift flour, cinnamon, and salt into a separate bowl and stir to combine. Add flour mixture to butter mixture and mix until combined. Press into a 10-by-15-inch baking pan. Brush the surface with egg white and sprinkle with chopped nuts. Bake for 45 minutes to 1 hour, or until set. Cut into 24 (approximately 2-1/4-inch) squares while hot.

24 SQUARES

ORANGE-SCENTED BISCOTTI

Biscotti are the ultimate dunking accompaniment for coffee because they're baked twice, so they don't fall apart in the liquid. To  toast almonds, spread on a baking sheet and bake at 350° for about 10 minutes, until golden, but not browned. Use a zester or a vegetable peeler to make orange zest, peeling off just the fragrant orange skin, not the bitter white pith.

3 cups all-purpose flour
1 cup granulated sugar
1/8 teaspoon salt
1 teaspoon baking powder
4 large eggs
1-1/2 teaspoons pure vanilla extract
1 teaspoon grated fresh orange zest

1-1/4 cup toasted almonds
Egg wash (1 egg mixed with 1 teaspoon
  water)
Raw sugar

Preheat oven to 325°. Line a baking sheet with parchment paper. Sift flour, sugar, salt, and baking powder into a medium bowl. Blend 4 eggs, vanilla extract, and orange zest in bowl of a mixer fitted with the paddle attachment. Add flour mixture and mix until dough forms. Add almonds just before dough comes together.

Divide dough into 4 equal pieces on a floured work surface. Shape each piece into a 10-inch by 2-inch log and flatten slightly. Place on the baking sheet, 2 inches apart. Brush with egg

wash and sprinkle with raw sugar. Bake for 25 minutes. Remove from oven and cool for 10 minutes. Place logs on a work surface and slice diagonally into 1-inch pieces.

Return biscotti to baking sheet, with cut side down. Reduce oven setting to 300° and bake for 35 to 38 minutes, turning them halfway through. Transfer to a wire rack to cool.

ABOUT 40 BISCOTTI

HUNGARIAN RUGELACH

1 cup (2 sticks) unsalted butter, softened
1/2 pound cream cheese, softened
1/4 teaspoon salt
2 cups sifted all-purpose flour
1 cup chopped walnuts
1/2 cup granulated sugar
1 tablespoon ground cinnamon

Mix butter, cream cheese, and salt in a bowl until creamy. Add flour, a little at a time, and mix to combine thoroughly. Shape into 12 to 14 balls. Place into a shallow dish, cover with plastic wrap and refrigerate overnight.

Flour a work surface lightly. Transfer balls to

the work surface and roll each into a 6-inch circle. Cut each into quarters.

Preheat oven to 325°. Mix nuts, sugar, and cinnamon until well blended. Drop 1 rounded teaspoon of the nut mixture onto each quarter-circle. Roll pointed edge of dough over filling. Pinch the edges of the dough together and shape into crescents. Place on 2 ungreased baking sheets, 3 inches apart, working in batches. Bake 1 sheet for about 12 minutes. Cool on the baking sheet for about 5 minutes and transfer to wire racks to cool completely. Repeat with remaining crescents, rotating the baking sheets.

48 TO 56 COOKIES

VIENNESE CRESCENTS

1 cup (2 sticks) unsalted butter, softened
1/3 cup granulated sugar
2/3 cup chopped almonds
1/4 teaspoon salt
2 cups all-purpose flour
Confectioners' sugar

Mix butter and sugar in a mixing bowl until creamy. Add almonds and salt and mix until combined. Using your hands, work the flour into the butter mixture. Cover with plastic wrap and refrigerate until chilled.

Preheat oven to 350°. Transfer dough to a work surface and pull off small pieces. Work with your hands until it is pliable but not sticky. Roll pieces between your palms to make pencil-thick strips and shape into small crescents. Place on 2 ungreased baking

sheets, about 3 inches apart, working in batches. Bake 1 sheet for about 12 minutes or until crescents are set but not browned. Cool for about 5 minutes on the baking sheet and transfer to wire racks to cool completely. Repeat with remaining crescents, rotating the baking sheets. Roll cooled crescents in confectioners' sugar.

75 CRESCENTS

SWEDISH SPRITZ COOKIES

1 cup (2 sticks) unsalted butter, softened
1 cup granulated sugar
1 egg, well beaten
1/4 teaspoon salt
2 teaspoons pure vanilla extract
2-1/2 cups all-purpose flour
Chocolate frosting, optional

Preheat oven to 350°. Mix butter and sugar in a large mixing bowl until very creamy. Add egg, salt, and vanilla and mix well to combine. Sift flour into butter mixture and mix to form a smooth dough. Roll out dough and use cookie cutters to make shapes or press it through a cookie press. Place cookies on 2 ungreased baking sheets, about 2 inches apart. Bake 1 sheet for 5 to 8 minutes or until lightly browned. Cool for about 5 minutes on the baking sheet and transfer to wire racks to cool completely. Repeat with remaining crescents, rotating baking sheets. If you wish, dip ends of cookies into chocolate frosting.

24 TO 36 COOKIES

APRICOT BARS

2/3 cup dried apricots
Nonstick vegetable oil spray for greasing
1/2 cup (1 stick) butter, softened
1/4 cup granulated sugar
1-1/3 cup all-purpose flour, sifted, divided
1/2 teaspoon baking powder
1/4 teaspoon salt
2 eggs
1 cup brown sugar
1/2 teaspoon pure vanilla extract
1/2 cup chopped walnuts
Confectioners' sugar

Rinse apricots, place them into a small saucepan with enough water to cover, and boil for 10 minutes. Drain. When cool enough to handle, chop coarsely.

To prepare crust, preheat oven to 350°. Grease a shallow 8-inch square pan. Combine butter, granulated

sugar, and 1 cup flour in a mixing bowl and, using your fingers or a fork, mix until combined and crumbly. Press into the prepared pan. Bake for about 25 minutes, or until lightly browned.

Meanwhile, prepare topping: sift 1/3 cup flour, baking powder and salt into a mixing bowl. In a separate bowl, beat eggs well. Gradually beat in brown sugar. Add flour mixture and mix well. Add vanilla, nuts, and apricots. When crust is baked, spread apricot mixture over it. Bake 30 minutes longer, or until done. Cool slightly in the pan. While still warm, cut into 32 (1-by-2-inch) bars. Pour confectioners' sugar into a shallow bowl or large plate and roll bars in it.

32 BARS

BEST-EVER BROWNIES

Nonstick vegetable oil spray or vegetable
* oil for greasing*
1/2 cup (1 stick) unsalted butter
4 squares (1-ounce each) unsweetened
* chocolate*
3 eggs
1-1/2 cups granulated sugar
1 teaspoon pure vanilla extract
1/4 teaspoon salt
3/4 cup sifted all-purpose flour
3/4 cup chopped pecans

Preheat oven to 350°. Spray or grease a 9-inch square pan. Melt butter and chocolate in a small, heavy saucepan set over low heat. Remove from heat and set aside to cool slightly.

Using an electric mixer set at medium speed, beat eggs in a large mixing bowl until foamy.

Gradually add sugar, vanilla, and salt, beating just until combined. Do not over-beat. Add flour gradually, and beat until just mixed. With a wooden spoon or rubber spatula, stir in pecans. Spoon batter into the prepared pan and smooth the top with a spatula.

Bake 30 to 35 minutes. The insides of the brownies should be soft and a toothpick inserted into the center should not come out completely clean.

Cool in the pan on a wire rack for about 30 minutes. Do not cut brownies while they are in the pan. Invert contents of the pan onto a wire rack to cool completely. When cool, refrigerate until chilled. When chilled, transfer to a cutting board and cut.

36 BROWNIES

Nut-Date Bars

Nonstick vegetable oil spray for greasing
3 eggs, separated
1 cup granulated sugar
1 cup all-purpose flour
1 teaspoon baking powder
Pinch of salt
1 cup walnuts, chopped
1 pound dates, pitted and quartered
Icing, next page

Preheat oven to 350°. Grease a shallow 8-inch square pan. Beat egg yolks and sugar in a large mixing bowl until creamy.

Sift flour, baking powder, and salt into another bowl and mix to combine. In a separate mixing bowl, beat egg whites until stiff. Using a rubber spatula, fold egg whites into yolk mixture, alternating with flour mixture. Add nuts and dates and mix to combine. Pour

into the prepared pan and smooth the surface with a knife. Bake for about 30 minutes. Cool in the pan, ice, and cut into 1-inch by 2-inch bars.

ICING

3/4 cup granulated sugar
Juice of 1/2 lemon

To prepare icing, combine sugar with lemon juice and stir until creamy.

32 BARS

VIENNESE SACHER TORTE

From one of the coffee capitals of the world comes this famous torte.

Butter and vegetable oil for greasing
3/4 cup (1-1/2 sticks) unsalted butter, softened
6 squares (1-ounce each) semisweet chocolate
3/4 cup granulated sugar
8 eggs, separated, plus whites of 2 eggs
1 cup all-purpose flour
2 tablespoons apricot jam
Chocolate Icing, next page

Preheat oven to 275°. Grease a 9-inch cake tin with a little butter and oil.

Using an electric mixer set at medium speed, beat butter in a mixing bowl until creamy. Melt chocolate in a small saucepan over low heat. Add chocolate and sugar to butter. Stir to blend thoroughly. Add 8 egg yolks, one at a time, beating between each addition. Add

 flour and beat until thoroughly incorporated. Stop the mixer and scrape the side of the bowl and beaters as needed.

Wash and dry beaters. Pour 10 egg whites into a large mixing bowl. With the mixer set at medium speed, beat egg whites until stiff peaks form. Fold egg whites into chocolate batter. Pour chocolate mixture into the prepared pan. Smooth with a knife. Bake for about 1 hour or until a toothpick inserted into the center comes out clean. Cool in the pan on a wire rack.

To assemble torte, cut cooled cake horizontally into 2 layers. Heat apricot jam slightly in a small saucepan set over medium heat or in a microwave. Spread half the jam on 1 cake layer; then place remaining cake layer on top. Spread it with remaining jam. Pour chocolate icing over the top and use a spatula to spread it so that it covers the entire torte.

CHOCOLATE ICING

1 cup water
1/3 cup granulated sugar
7 squares (1-ounce each) semisweet chocolate

Pour water into a small saucepan, add sugar and cook, stirring with a wooden spoon, until sugar is dissolved and forms a thin thread when you dip a wooden spoon into it and then lift it up out of the pot.

Melt chocolate in another small saucepan over low heat. Add sugar syrup to chocolate. Stir until it coats the back of a spoon.

8 SERVINGS

CHOCOLATE PECAN PIE

1 unbaked Chocolate Crumb Pie Crust,
  next page
1-1/2 squares (1-ounce each) unsweetened
  chocolate
3 tablespoons unsalted butter
3 eggs, beaten
1 cup granulated sugar
1/2 cup corn syrup
1 cup pecans, coarsely chopped
Real Whipped Cream to taste, page 160,
  optional

Preheat oven to 400°. Prepare Chocolate Crumb Pie Crust, but do not bake.

Melt chocolate and butter in a saucepan set over low heat. Remove from heat and slowly

add eggs, stirring constantly. Add sugar and corn syrup and beat until combined. Stir in pecans. Pour into pie crust and bake for 10 minutes.

Reduce oven temperature to 350° and bake for 30 to 35 minutes longer. Transfer to a wire rack to cool slightly. Serve hot or cold. If you wish, top with whipped cream.

6 TO 8 SERVINGS

CHOCOLATE CRUMB PIE CRUST

Nonstick vegetable oil spray or vegetable oil
  for greasing
1-1/2 cups finely crushed chocolate wafers
3 tablespoons granulated sugar
1/2 teaspoon ground cinnamon
1/3 cup unsalted butter, melted

Preheat oven to 350°. Lightly grease a 9-inch springform pan or pie plate. Combine crushed wafers, sugar, and cinnamon in a mixing bowl. Add melted butter and mix well. Press mixture into the bottom of prepared pan and 1 inch up the side, flattening it with the back of a spoon. Bake for 8 to 10 minutes. Cool completely on a wire rack.

REAL WHIPPED CREAM

Real coffee creations and baked goods deserve real whipped cream. And it's easy. If you must work in advance, cover it with plastic wrap and refrigerate; then whisk a bit if necessary just before serving. If you need more than this recipe makes, adjust the ingredients proportionately. And don't over-mix or you'll make butter.

1 cup cold heavy cream
2 teaspoons granulated sugar or to taste

Chill the beaters of an electric mixer. Pour cream into a chilled mixing bowl. Mix at low speed until cream is thickened. Add sugar and mix until soft peaks form.

2 TO 2-1/2 CUPS